AMBITIOUS
BUT RUBBISH

The secrets behind Top Gear's craziest creations

Richard Porter

CONTENTS

INTRODUCTION

Since not even the dodgiest of dealers would buy them, we've collected a selection of the battered, modified and generally ruined cars featured in this book and put them on display in the World of Top Gear, at the National Motor Museum, Beaulieu, Hampshire. Seeing really is believing when it comes to this five bob assortment of automotive angle iron.

TOP GEAR is more than just a programme

about cars. It's a programme about asking questions no one else has asked, about mucking around because you can, about the dangerously stupid recesses of the male brain. It's a programme that acknowledges the most dangerous words in the English language are 'Watch this!' It's also a programme that freely accepts the idea that failure is funny. In fact, it thrives on it.

This last point makes *Top Gear* almost unique. When other television programmes are being made, if something goes wrong or if a presenter messes up a simple task and is made to look foolish, the director shouts 'cut' and they do it all again. On *Top Gear*, when something doesn't work out the way it was supposed to and the presenter is left looking like an idiot, the director leaves the cameras running in the knowledge that this is the kind of moment that makes the programme what it is.

Top Gear is often approached by out-take shows and asked to supply hilarious left overs from a secret stash of error ridden footage in the edit suite. Every time this happens, it has to be met with an apology and an explanation that actually *Top Gear* doesn't really have out-takes. If it goes wrong, it's in the programme. And it's usually one of the most memorable moments too.

Because *Top Gear* is just about the only TV programme that likes to put its darkest moments and its biggest failures on screen, you would assume there's not much that even the casual viewer won't know about what happened whilst filming a given episode. There are, however, many stories to be told about the original thinking behind many of the show's most memorable moments, about how they were filmed and about the parts that had to be cut out for reasons of length, decency or because the BBC didn't like them. This book tells those stories.

THE INDESTRUCTIBLE HILUX

Series 3, episode 5
First transmitted: 23 November 2009
Filming locations: Bristol;
the Top Gear test track, Surrey;
Hackney, London.

THE idea behind one of *Top Gear*'s most memorable items formed many years earlier when the show's executive producer, Andy Wilman, suffered a hire-car mix-up in Dubai and, to his irritation, was given the keys to an ancient Hilux. His mood quickly changed when he discovered this creaking pick-up was unstoppable and could rampage around the desert rescuing other cars from the sand. This story came as no surprise to Jeremy, who had noticed that whenever TV news footage showed rebel fighters overthrowing governments in Africa and the Middle East, they were always doing it with just two things: AK-47s and tatty Hiluxes. The idea of testing a Toyota to destruction was born.

A likely example was found on *Auto Trader* and was in such shabby condition that even the man selling it couldn't believe someone was willing to pay good money for his rusty, dirty, strange-smelling farm hack. Little did he realise that it would become a TV star. Jeremy started his destruction test by pitting the Hilux against the sturdy city of Bristol and, frankly,

things went rather badly. But only for Bristol. The Toyota's tow bar made a bit of a mess of some flagstones as it drove down a set of steps, and the vicar into whose tree it was crashed got rather cross about the scuff marks on his bark, but the Hilux was unbowed. So Clarkson took it down to the Severn Estuary, home of the second-greatest tide in the

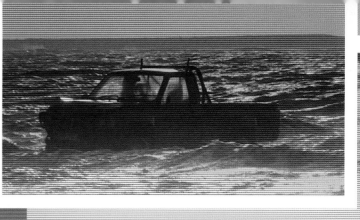

world, and tried to drown it. This didn't go entirely to plan. As the mighty flow of water swept in, the tethers holding the Hilux in place broke and the local lifeboat crew reckoned the plucky Toyota would be swept miles out to sea. Standing on the shore, Clarkson began composing a closing piece to camera in which he would solemnly confess that *Top Gear* had not only destroyed a Toyota Hilux, they had also lost it. Only when the tide receded did the glorious truth emerge; instead of drifting out to sea, the Toyota had dug into the thick sand of the seabed. It was probably dead, but at least we had the body. When it was hauled onto dry land, things didn't look good. The interior was full of silt, the windscreen

had popped out, and the engine was waterlogged. Jeremy composed another solemn piece announcing the Toyota's death and delivered it to camera.

His sombre words were, as it turned out, premature. Just moments later, the Hilux coughed back into life. The gap from being hauled onto dry land to that first successful crank of the starter was less than an hour. There was no TV trickery, no cunning sleight of hand, no army of technicians. A determined Toyota mechanic called Andy had revived the sodden Hilux using only a bag of tools and a can of WD-40.

When the call came through to the *Top Gear* office to say that the Hilux wasn't dead, the production team could barely believe it. Clearly, more tests

would have to be devised. And still the Hilux shrugged them off. Especially the wrecking ball, which actually didn't work as well as imagined because the crane it was attached to couldn't spin around fast enough to get a really violent whack against the Toyota's crumbling bodywork. In the end, Clarkson resorted to setting the poor thing on fire, but even that couldn't stop it, though it did render the 1980s-spec interior plastics poisonously untouchable.

Jeremy had failed to kill the Hilux. So then James had a go. A demolition company offered to put the pick-up on top of a tower block and then dynamite the building, boldly claiming that their explosives

were so accurate they could predict not just where the Toyota would land, but which way up. They were, as it turns out, a bit wrong on that score. The Hilux came to rest belly up and peppered with bits of old concrete. Yet after a digger had clawed it down from the rubble pile, our ace Toyota tech Andy got it going again in less than five minutes. It was incredible.

Throughout this endeavour he had used nothing more than a bag of tools, and the only 'spare part' fitted was an old Fairy Liquid bottle fashioned into a water tank. The old Toyota simply could not be stopped.

After that, it seemed pointless to keep trying to destroy a truly indestructible car and the Hilux was given pride of place on a plinth.

THE CAR TRAINS

Series 17, episode 4

First transmitted: 17 July 2011

Filming locations:
The Great Central Railway, Leicestershire.

THE car-and-caravan trains is a *Top Gear* item that might never have happened. The slot it filled in the 17th series was originally occupied by a grand plan to build a better, cheaper, more manoeuvrable fire engine. Many ideas were bandied around – motorbike fire engines, sports car fire engines, something involving a Bedford Rascal – but none quite made sense. The truth is, the fire engines that already exist are actually pretty hard to improve on and, until *Top Gear* could think of a way to make them better, the idea was shelved. This left a nasty gap in the series planner. Happily, at this point a letter arrived in the office from a viewer with an interesting idea – trains made from cars. He'd even included a rough photo mock-up of his plan. The idea was bandied around the office. The high cost of new rail projects and the ever-increasing price of train fares are always

in the news. Large-engined second-hand cars are cheap because fewer people want them these days. Combine the two and you've got a perfect cost-effective way to make the railways relevant again. There was just one thing left to find out; would it actually work?

As often happens with things that seem like a good idea in the *Top Gear* office, no one had a clue if the on-paper brilliance of car trains would translate into anything more than a big heap of swearing, skinned knuckles and a total waste of time. Some railway boffins were consulted. Strangely, they'd never tried making a train out of a car and, as a result, they couldn't say if it would work either. The only solution was to get out there and do it.

In principle, Jeremy's choice of a Jaguar XJS made sense. A big, powerful V12 engine was just what a car train would need, and it didn't even matter that for

some reason he'd decided to go for the convertible model. Better yet, the Jag's chassis was almost exactly the right width for a British rail track. In fact, it's staggering how little work was needed to turn a wafty old sports car into a working locomotive. Well, almost working. On a section of railway certified for testing real trains, the rear-wheel-drive Jag train couldn't get enough grip to pull the caravan carriages behind it. A small argument broke out.

James quickly did some research and concluded that the problem could be solved using a four-wheel-drive car. And the four-wheel-drive car that offered the most power for the money was an old Audi S8.

Jeremy, meanwhile, had discovered that the Jaguar was more than capable of pulling a single 'carriage' with ease, and then lopped the caravan's roof off to create his 'sports train'. Incredibly, both trains

TOP FACT

For series 18, the TGV12 sports train was made part of the Top Gear studio set. Keen-eyed viewers may notice that in later episodes its bucket seats went missing. That's because Jeremy nicked them for his cut-price rally-cross BMW.

actually seemed to work. Which was fortunate because *Top Gear* had invited some of the railways world's biggest names to join the presenters on their inaugural journeys, all of whom seemed slightly baffled by the whole endeavour.

In fact, the man from the train magazine who rode in Jeremy's open-top carriage may have been scarred for life by his experiences. This wasn't an easy item to film. When *Top Gear* shoot cars it's always possible for the camera tracking-car to get past the subject matter to pick up more shots and the crew can always turn around or stop their car if need be. This isn't possible on a railway, especially when there are other trains coming in the opposite direction.

However, it was worth doing if only to prove that, with a few minor teething problems, trains made from cars can work. Sort of.

£100 CARS

Series 14, episode 3

First transmitted: 23 May 2004

Filming locations:
Toddington Services, Bedfordshire;
M1 and M6 motorways;
Old Trafford Stadium, Manchester;
the Top Gear test track, Surrey.

THIS was the very first time *Top Gear* sent the three presenters out to buy three old cars and then set them a series of challenges. It was inspired by two things; firstly, criticism that the show featured too many expensive, impractical supercars, and secondly, an ongoing fascination with how much car you could get for how little money. However, until it was filmed and edited, no one knew whether the idea of Jeremy, Richard and James going on a road trip and undertaking a series of tests together – now a staple part of the programme – would actually work.

Finding the cars was surprisingly easy. Hammond and May bought theirs sight-unseen off the internet. Richard got seduced by the GTi badge on his Rover and only later discovered the rusting bodywork, gaffer-taped sunroof and missing radio. May sidestepped the rust issue by buying a fully galvanised Audi and was staggered at how tidy his car was when he collected it. Clarkson acquired his Volvo by different means.

After taking the family XC90 for a service, his wife had noticed the ageing 760 in the dealer's yard and

mentioned to Jeremy that, as an almost worthless part-exchange, it would soon be dispatched to the scrap yard. To avoid any chance of the price being jacked up in the presence of a man off the telly, Jeremy sent his wife back to the Volvo garage and instructed her to offer them £1 for it. Amazingly, they accepted.

The other two presenters had no idea how little he'd paid until the final scoring in the studio.

By the standards of later *Top Gear* journeys, a drive to Manchester and back wasn't very exciting but it proved that all three cars worked well, despite costing less than a return train ticket. The excitement came later when all three were crashed into specially built – and worryingly solid – breeze block walls. BBC Health & Safety took a lot of persuading on that one. These days, the cars the presenters buy are shuffled off to a museum when filming is over, but back then no one could find any use for the plucky cut-price trio and they were donated to the local fire brigade, who cut them up during accident-rescue training. So at least they didn't die in vain.

POLICE CARS

Series II, episode I

First transmitted: 22 June 2008

Filming locations:
The Top Gear Technology Centre, Oxfordshire; the Top Gear test track, Surrey.

JEREMY had long been complaining about those TV shows called things like *Stop! Cops! Kaboom!* that show real-life police chases from around the world. Specifically, he hated the way footage from America always ended with a cop smashing a Ford Crown Vic into an exploding petrol station whilst clips from British chases inevitably recorded a bobby in a diesel Astra driving very slowly over a kerb. The problem, he decided, was that our police paid too much for their cars and were therefore scared of damaging them. If the cars were cheaper they wouldn't be afraid of wrecking them and Brit cops wouldn't look so useless on international television. An idea was born. Armed

with no more than £1,000, the presenters would each buy what they believed to be the ideal, bargain-priced car for the police forces of Great Britain.

Mindful of the need to shine on *Crash! Wallop! Arrest!*-type programmes, Jeremy went for a blend of power and style. James remembered that the American police drive big, V8-powered rear-wheel-drive saloons and

picked one of those. Richard got distracted thinking about police Range Rovers and bought what he foolishly believed to be a 'cut-price' version.

The presenters were then given £500 to turn what they'd bought into convincing police cars. Around this time, Jeremy was completely obsessed with a minty green paint that Skoda offered on its Fabia

hatchback and painted his 'stylish' police car in this colour. Later in the same series he used the leftover paint during the cheap Alfas challenge. James, meanwhile, hatched an ingenious plan to paint one side of his Lexus like a brick wall to enable him to 'go undercover' in urban areas, before abandoning this plan on grounds of cost, complexity and because it would be completely useless in any situation where there wasn't a brick wall to park up against. Instead, he picked a classic British police-car colour scheme and fulfilled his urban stealth idea with a subterfuge based around ice-cream van chimes. Finally, Hammond was very proud of his 'stinger' system and his high-visibility blue light strategy. Even though the

After the police cars item had been made, the cars were mothballed until James decided he would like to make his grand entrance onto the stage at the Top Gear Live show in his Lexus LS400. It was dug out of a museum and, predictably, started first time.

'stinger' was useless and the masses of blue lights totally overwhelmed the car's electrical system, making it conk out all the time.

In principle, the cheap police cars idea was a good one. In practice it was, frankly, rubbish. James's immobilising paint-spray system could be vanquished with a simple flick of the wipers and Jeremy's Boudicca spike system caused the entire wheel to become detached, almost took out one of the cameramen and caused some stern words from BBC Health & Safety. Worse yet, because Richard fudged the numbers and then ate the score sheet, *Top Gear* had to declare that the best car for the British police was a Suzuki Vitara with a doormat on the front. Sorry.

REASONABLY PRICED CAR 1 THE SUZUKI LIANA

Series 1–7

First transmitted: 2002

THE idea of the Reasonably Priced Car came from an obsession in the *Top Gear* office with seeing glamorous celebrities in the kind of unglamorous, workaday cars they'd never normally drive. For some reason, executive producer Andy Wilman was particularly fixated with the idea of Bryan Ferry in a cheap hatchback.

The idea was agreed but before the very first series of new *Top Gear* went into production, a car had to be found for the star guests to drive. A list was drawn up of things that might legitimately be called 'reasonably priced' and from that list Hyundai seemed a good bet. Sadly, their PR people were having none of it, and nor were most other carmakers.

Only Suzuki showed any interest and agreed to send a Liana to the *Top Gear* office for assessment. When it was delivered, Jeremy and some of the production team went outside to have a look. With howls of laughter they stared at this strange blue saloon with its gawky looks, its plastic-looking interior and its inexplicably massive ignition key that looked like a blunt sword. Even the name, purported to be a contraction of 'life in a new age', was fantastically absurd. But it had an engine, it had brakes, it was to all intents and purposes a car and, at £9,995 on the

road, it was without question reasonably priced. With no other carmaker playing ball, the Liana was given the nod.

At this point, Suzuki themselves had doubts. Reinvented *Top Gear* was an unknown quantity at that point and the company's bosses were worried that this could all backfire. In the end, their PR man put his neck on the line and said if it didn't work out, they could reward him with a trip to the job centre. He needn't have worried. The Liana – actually two Lianas, after a back-up car was introduced in 2003 – became almost as big a star as the people who drove it. The lead car has just 7,000 miles on the clock yet

Suzuki's boffins calculate that this is equivalent to 140,000 miles of normal road driving, and in all of those laps it's never given any trouble. We'll overlook the times when the pressure of extreme cornering prompted the wheel nuts to tear through the standard steel wheels, causing Lionel Richie, Trevor Eve and (unseen on TV) Ian Wright to tripod onto the grass. *Top Gear* moved on to the Lacetti and then the Cee'd but the Liana is still wheeled out whenever F1 drivers are on the show, in order to keep the separate pro-driver lap-board fair. It'll always be the original – and probably the *Top Gear* team's favourite – Reasonably Priced Car.

ON paper, the snowbine was another brilliantly simple *Top Gear* idea. Every winter the newspapers report that Britain is thrown into 'snow chaos' whilst at the same time the countryside is full of combine harvesters sitting idle and waiting for summer. Why not make them earn their keep all year round by turning them into snowploughs?

Like so many of the presenters' ideas, this one sounded flawless. But, since no one had ever attempted it before, the only way to find out if it worked in real life would be to crack on and do it. With the aid of a slightly bemused agricultural engineering company, Jeremy, Richard and James set to work and a short time later the snowbine was

ready. In principle, it seemed to be good. Yes, the grit cannon was a bit aggressive and needed to be wound back whenever it wasn't being used for fear that it would accidentally machine-gun someone to death with small stones, but in theory the rest of it was a success. In practice, however, no one could say, since at the time of filming Britain remained conspicuously snow-free. Even a plan to take the Snowbine to Scotland was aborted when it seemed bitter winter weather was far from guaranteed. The only answer was to ship the newly created machine to the very definitely snowy landscape of Norway. This seemed simple enough but when the ferry carrying the lorry with the Snowbine on the back

After filming, the Snowbine was shipped back to Britain and stored in the car park at the back of Top Gear's studio production office. Come studio recording day, it took a great deal of coaxing back to life and eventually spluttered into action with an enormous cloud of diesel fumes that engulfed the entire area and put everyone off their breakfast.

arrived at a Norwegian port, a mix-up with the paperwork saw it impounded by the authorities who wrongly believed someone was attempting to illegally import a piece of agricultural equipment (that had, of course, inexplicably been converted to work as a snowplough). There was a very real risk that the Snowbine would be sent home without ever touching actual snow. After some frantic 3 a.m. phone calls, the mighty machine was released and reunited with the presenters the next day. Although they might have wished it hadn't been when they ventured onto a frozen lake and felt the ice cracking beneath the weight of its enormous wheels. You might notice that at the

end of the ice-runway sequence some of the filming isn't quite as steady as usual and the presenters' reactions seem a little panicked. Both are testament to the moment of sheer panic when the landing light aircraft went out of control and crashed into a bank of snow. It was a genuine heart-in-the-mouth moment, especially for one of *Top Gear*'s cameramen who was on board the plane at the time. That aside, the expedition to Norway was a great success and proved that a snowplough made from a combine harvester is basically an ingenious idea.

Although, strangely, no one has yet contacted the *Top Gear* office to ask for the blueprints.

MOTORHOMES

Series 15, episode 4

First transmitted: 18 July 2010

Filming locations:
Fleet Services, Hampshire; M3 motorway;
Polzeath, Cornwall.

IT seemed like a good idea at the time. Rid Britain of the caravan menace by making motorhomes that are cool enough to be appealing and compact enough to fit down UK roads. Unfortunately, it was downhill from there. Richard sat in the *Top Gear* office drawing elaborate sketches of a massive fold-out house on the back of a Land Rover, little realising that his on-paper ingenuity would have weighed 50 tons in real life. That is, unless all the walls and ceilings were made of very thin metal sheeting and corrugated plastic that would clatter when it was moving and blow away when it was static.

James looked to have drawn on his passion for aeronautical engineering to good effect with a clever, lightweight roof-box that used sound aviation principles in its construction. Unfortunately, it was also uncomfortably cramped and smelt like an old attic full of damp carpets and petrol.

The greatest buffoonery, however, came from

TOP FACT

The pig-headed presenters became fixated on finding specific cars for this challenge, all of which proved tricky to source within budget. Jeremy's Citroen and James's Lotus were especially hard to find in decent nick, and the ones they bought went wrong before filming had even started.

Clarkson, who had been watching a lot of *Grand Designs* the week this challenge came through and concocted a preposterous tower-block affair that he sincerely believed would work as long as he plonked it on top of a car with self-levelling, fluid-based suspension. After much searching on the internet, he bought an old Citroen CX estate and rapidly discovered that he couldn't have provided a less stable foundation for his three-storey building if he'd constructed it on top of a trampoline.

If you look closely during this film, you might notice a blue VW camper van in the back of some shots. It was a forfeit car provided by the producers to be used in the event that any of the presenters admitted defeat with their own motorhomes. However, in an already lengthy feature, all reference to it was cut out to save time. Nonetheless, it's a miracle Jeremy, Richard and James weren't begging to sleep in it after the first night because frankly their own efforts were rubbish.

TOP GEAR

had long harboured a desire to film in India. Jeremy and James had both been there in the past and were very keen to return to this uniquely colourful and interesting country. So when, in July 2010, Prime Minister David Cameron paid a visit to India and declared that the UK should become its 'partner of choice' for trade, the seeds of an idea were sown. Further investigation revealed that Anglo-Indian trade could indeed do with a boost. In fact, Britain does more trade with Ireland than it does with India, and even the Belgians enjoy a more prosperous

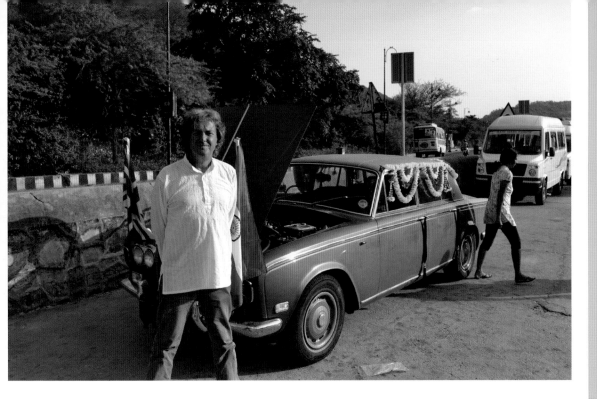

trading relationship with the vast sub-continent. The plan was simple. Get out there in three old British cars and drum up some business for UK plc. Research quickly showed that the choice of British cars available on the ground in India was not good, unless Jeremy, Richard and James all wanted to buy identical examples of the locally-made Hindustan Ambassador, based on the British-designed Morris Oxford. Buying the cars at home would give far greater choice, and normally in the face of choice the presenters naturally go in wildly different directions. Initially, that was the case here too. Jeremy was very keen on a Jag, even considering

an old Mk X from the 1960s, which was as wide and imposing as a Georgian house. He settled instead for an XJS whilst Hammond eyed up Minis and May pondered the possibility of getting a Rolls-Royce within budget. This seemed eminently possible, but then James had a change of heart and also started mumbling about buying a Mini. Since *Top Gear* road trips tend to work best when the presenters are in a trio of very different cars – leading to very different problems and giving the whole thing an amusing, raggle-taggle, Bash Street Kids sort of appearance – the producers gently persuaded James that his first idea was better. Happily, he agreed.

TOP FACT *Top Gear specials had slowly grown from one hour to an hour and a quarter. The producers had always resisted going up to a full hour and a half because that's a long time to ask people to watch three silly men mucking about. However, the India Special proved impossible to get below that length, largely because to cut out any of the key scenes would have led to bizarre continuity errors, leaving viewers wondering why, for example, there were inexplicable musical instruments strapped to the cars.*

So it was that the three cars were found, collected and crated up for their long journey to India. What was amazing about them is just how well they fared in the harsh conditions encountered on the road trip. It was baking hot for much of the journey and, in *Top Gear*'s experience of old cars, that usually means at least one of them overheating every five miles. It's something that starts out as amusing television and ends up being a bloody inconvenience if you're trying to get anywhere. But the Jaguar, the Mini and the Rolls were, by and large, extremely hardy and made it through the searing cauldron of the sub-continent without

boiling over, until they reached the other extreme in the bitter cold of the Himalayas. They were fine in the mountains, too. The presenters? Less so. It was here, as they camped one night in the freezing cold, that Jeremy heard a tiny shivering voice emerging from James's sleeping bag. 'Jeremy....,' it said. Clarkson knew there was a problem; May never calls him Jeremy. 'Jeremy... I'm very unhappy.'

Nonetheless, the trio made it to the very apex of the road that links India and China, at which point they decided the best thing they could do was to leave their proud cars on plinths to serve as a reminder to all

those passing between these two flourishing economic superpowers that there is a faraway place called Great Britain. However, shortly after this stirring monument was finished a man came along and pointed out that the patriotic monument had been constructed in an area of supreme religious and spiritual significance and it had to be removed immediately. Which is why you won't find the India Special cars on the road from India to China any more. They're actually in a museum in Hampshire. Which, on the plus side, does make it rather more convenient if you want to see them. Especially for people in Wimborne Minster.

THE BMW 330D 24-HOUR RACER

Series 10, episode 9

First transmitted: 9 December 2007

Filming locations: The Top Gear Technology Centre, Didcot, Oxfordshire; Silverstone Circuit, Northamptonshire.

Ambitious But Rubbish

THE idea of going 24-hour racing came about after the *Top Gear* tractoring challenge in which the presenters planted a field of rape seed and then discovered that their crop was suitable only for making eco diesel. What better way to get rid of it than by driving round and round in circles non-stop for one whole day? They just needed a well-balanced, powerful yet affordable diesel saloon, which turned out to be a BMW 330D.

James was busy poncing about drinking wine with Oz Clarke so Jeremy and Richard went down to the Top Gear Technology Centre and set about prepping the car. This wasn't entirely straightforward, not only because of their basic level of buffoonery but also because the electronics on a modern car are so complicated and so completely interlinked that attempting to remove something as simple as the interior light can cause the entire computer system to throw a fit and immobilise the engine.

Nonetheless, they worked round these problems and a surprisingly passable racer emerged on the other side. All it needed was some stickers to really look the part. Sadly, BBC regulations ruled out the possibility of using real companies' names so fake sponsors were confected instead. And for comic effect, these were worked out in Adobe Photoshop using a profile picture of a 3-series

TOP FACT

Some thought was given to removing the indestructible Toyota Hilux from the plinth at the back of the Top Gear studio and putting this BMW in its place. In the end, however, it was agreed that the Hilux was just too iconic and therefore irreplaceable.

so that they might say silly things when the doors were opened. One of Jeremy's suggestions was based around a town in north Lincolnshire and would have meant the passenger door could not be opened in polite company. The car was a surprisingly effective racer, but that's nothing to the surprise of discovering that our boys could actually hold their own on the track. Yes, James was a little bit steady, Richard was a little bit aggressive and Jeremy sometimes got carried away but, with able back-up from The Stig to make up some of the time they lost, *Team Top Gear* put on a good showing in what turned out to be tough conditions. Even when the homemade diesel started eating through the seals on the fuel line, our plucky mechanics worked tirelessly to bodge around the problem and keep the BMW going. No one actually expected Clarkson, Hammond and May to a) take a race that seriously and b) actually finish it. But, amazingly, they did and Jeremy's reaction at the end says it all. He might have subsequently claimed that he had a lash in his eye or that it was just his cheeks were 'a bit sweaty' but everyone knew the real story. It had been emotional.

AMPHIBIOUS CARS 1

Series 8, episode 3

First transmitted: 21 May 2006

Filming locations: Hilperton, Wiltshire;
Southampton, Hampshire;
Keele Services, Staffordshire;
Newcastle-under-Lyme, Staffordshire;
Rudyard Lake, Staffordshire.

IN the run up to *Top Gear* series eight, the presenters got to talking about amphibious cars and, specifically, how none of the water-going machines to date had quite captured the world's imagination. The three of them decided they could do better.

As is often the case with these challenges, Clarkson, Hammond and May naturally came up with very different ideas. Jeremy decided to base his on a Toyota Hilux (which was a good idea) and became obsessed with making as few boat-related additions as possible (which wasn't). Richard, because he likes outdoorsy stuff, went for a camper van, which he would force into unholy union with a canal boat. James surprised everyone with his sailing-boat scheme, to be based on an ancient and rather shabby Triumph Herald that appeared to be listing to one side even when it was on dry land. Professional boat-makers and salty seadogs were consulted during the build process for all three

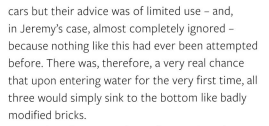

cars but their advice was of limited use – and, in Jeremy's case, almost completely ignored – because nothing like this had ever been attempted before. There was, therefore, a very real chance that upon entering water for the very first time, all three would simply sink to the bottom like badly modified bricks.

It was, therefore, something of a surprise when May, Clarkson and Hammond drove nervously into Rudyard Lake and actually stayed afloat. For a bit.

The truth is that Richard was doomed from the off because his propeller smashed on the entry ramp and broke. The Dampervan's engine, which had been fitted in a panic the night before after the original engine suffered catastrophic failure, gave out in sympathy and he was going nowhere. Not that it really mattered because the whole thing was rapidly filling with water and within minutes was heading to the bottom. On TV, we then saw Richard catching a lift with Jeremy whilst

behind the scenes the production team suddenly realised that, to get the damn thing out of the lake, they needed to attach a rope to it. Which was a problem, because it was now completely under water. As if by magic, a hulk of a man appeared from nowhere, declared himself the local open-water swimming champion, offered to jump into the freezing water in nothing more than his smalls and dived under to lash a rope to the stricken VW. Without his help, the Dampervan might still be under there. And it might have had a frozen *Top Gear* researcher stuck to it.

Back on top of the lake it seemed that, against the odds, Jeremy's pick-up and James's sailing Herald were actually working. Sort of. That is until Clarkson, the scent of amphibious victory in his nostrils, pulled an over-ambitious turn before the finish and his Toybota became the wrong way up. Captain Aqua Slow sailed in and won the race, or at least claimed that he did even though the

Herald's clutch gave out and it couldn't reverse up the ramp.

It was easy enough to pull the little Triumph onto dry land and with Hammond's van now retrieved from the water as well, there was just the small matter of extracting Jeremy's Hilux from the lake. This was harder than you might think because Clarkson had packed every cavity and compartment with foam and, whilst it's very good for making things buoyant, foam doesn't really care which way up it floats. Without any momentum behind it, getting the Toyota the right way up so it could be hauled from the water took ages, but once it was back on land a most amazing thing happened. The same technician who had worked on the indestructible Hilux in an earlier series came along and, using just his usual bag of basic tools and his trusty can of WD-40, he got the sodden pick-up started again. Which just goes to prove once more that you can't kill a Toyota Hilux. Even one that's been turned into a bad boat.

CARAVAN AIRSHIP

Series 14, episode 3

First transmitted: 19 November 2009

Filming location: Cardington, Bedfordshire;
Norwich Airport, Norfolk;
most of Eastern England, frankly.

Microlite Discovery

THE idea came from the aeronautical and rather strange brain of James May, who thought of the concept during an idle moment in the *Top Gear* office and began sketching what he had in mind on a whiteboard. The executive producer looked at the proposal with scepticism. 'If that works,' he said, 'I promise you, I'll eat my own genitals.' And following that unusual wager, he agreed to let James go off and make his deranged drawings into reality.

This wasn't as easy as May first thought because, whilst caravans are light, they aren't quite light enough to work with the size and type of airship gasbag James could afford to have made. The obvious answer would be to strip out the entire interior, but since this creation had to work as a caravan when it arrived at its destination, that simply wouldn't do. Instead, May set about locating the heaviest parts – the bed, the kitchenette and so on – and then cleverly lightened them using aerospace

materials. He even considered filling the caravan's tyres with helium, which is lighter than normal air, until he worked out that the potential weight saving was microscopic. He also had to ditch a hare-brained idea in which the gas burner for the airship could be flipped round and used as a hob in the kitchen, realising it would probably sear his face off.

With the help of some professional airship-builders who took care of unusual obstacles like getting the caravan registered as a legitimate aircraft, the parts

of May's mad plan came together. There was a delay in getting everything put together as *Take That* were occupying the hangar. But once Gary Barlow and his mates had finished rehearsing their stadium tour, the caravan airship could be assembled.

Finally, the day of truth arrived. James's airship would fly for the first time. Except it was too windy and it didn't. The production team got bored, wandered into the next-door hangar, which houses the enormous Gotham City set used in Batman films, and received a

bit of a telling-off from security. Eventually everyone went home. A few days later conditions were perfect and with a jaunty wave, May clambered into his caravan and, to everyone's amazement, successfully took off. A stupid doodle on a whiteboard had become reality and, by golly, it actually worked. Sort of. There were what James would call 'directional control issues', but the fact is that the caravan airship flew. Yet strangely, the executive producer still hasn't gone through with his part of the wager.

STRETCHED LIMOS

Series 9, episode 6

First transmitted: 4 March 2007

Filming locations: High Wycombe, Buckinghamshire; the Top Gear test track, Surrey; west London.

MOST stretched limos in Britain are based on massive American cars like Lincolns and Hummers. The presenters thought this was stupid and were sent away to come up with alternatives based on models readily available in the UK. Their solutions were, to say the least, innovative. Jeremy started with an old Fiat Panda, reasoning that its smallness didn't matter since it would be made bigger in the stretching process and its tiny engine was irrelevant when most limousines spend their time crawling through cities. Richard employed the same logic that had created the convertible people-carrier – there's never been a car like this – to come up with the concept of a sports limo. And James used his extensive knowledge of car-industry platform-sharing to formulate a push-me-pull-you limo based on the visually different but mechanically almost identical Saab 9000 and Alfa 164.

Putting these unusual ideas into practice was a fascinating challenge. Jeremy got so excited by his freshly-severed Panda that he ran a tube from the fuel line into a plastic container of petrol and wasted an afternoon zooming up and down a private road in the front section of his Fiat. He also couldn't resist adding more and more length to his design until he realised he'd need a second rear axle to take the weight and had to buy another rotting Panda to cannibalise. This second car's lights and dashboard were later fished from a mound of junk at the Top Gear Technology Centre and used in the Hammerhead-i Eagle Thrust electric car. Meanwhile, Richard discovered that stretching a mid-engined car meant extending not just the radiator plumbing, the brake lines and the throttle cable but also, in the case of the MGF with its fluid-based Hydragas chassis, the complicated pipes that made the suspension work. And James rapidly realised that the Saab and the Alfa weren't as similar under the skin as he'd fondly imagined.

The three limos had to be approved by government inspectors before they would be allowed on the road and, amazingly, once Jeremy had taken a chunk out of his giant Panda and James had fitted a better locking mechanism to his Alfa's front wheels, they were certified as road-legal and ready to chauffeur some top pop celebrities to the Brit Awards. This didn't go well. Jeremy's ridiculous Fiat brought half of west London to a halt, Richard's MG left Jamelia not only embarrassed but also deafened by the jammed throttle of the engine behind her and, whilst James's limo worked reasonably well, May's directional ineptitude brought even nice guy Lemar to the end of his tether. Up until that point, it was easily the most chaos *Top Gear* had ever caused during filming. No wonder British limo companies continue to stick with imported American designs.

THE SKI JUMP MINI

Top Gear Winter Olympics
First transmitted: 12 February 2006
Filming location: Lillehammer, Norway

THE *Top Gear* Winter Olympics had been going well. James had smashed up the only production-spec Audi Q7 in Europe, Richard had crashed his Suzuki Swift ice hockey car and Jeremy had machine-gunned a tree to death. But apart from those minor problems, it was a great success. The final challenge, however, threatened to test our boys' ingenuity and grit to the limit. It was, as Hammond said at the time, 'the cutting-edge of cocking about'. Their objective was simple – get an old-school Mini to leap from the actual ski-jump used in the 1994 Winter Olympics and to fly further than a real ski-jumping

man. After a frankly baffling lecture from James involving lots of letters and something about parabolas, it was clear that only one organisation could save this endeavour from certain failure – the Rocket Men. The Rocket Men may be based in a shed in Glossop and they may only practise rocketry during evenings and weekends, but never underestimate these quietly nerdy Northerners because they really do know their stuff. They quickly yet precisely calculated how much thrust the Mini would need and worked out, to the exact millimetre, the angle the rockets would need to be at to provide maximum thrust and much-

needed stability. The three rockets on the back may have appeared to poke out in different and totally cock-eyed directions, but that was actually the result of detailed calculations aimed at making the Mini fly straight and level and not into the local post office. If they'd got it wrong, there was a very real chance that the little red car would have flown wildly out of control and smashed into Lillehammer town centre. Which would have taken some explaining.

There was much hilarity in the workshop at the contrast between the boffins' microscopically detailed work, which really was rocket science, and

the clonking artlessness of Jeremy's ski construction, which really was a load of crudely-welded pig iron. Despite the Rocketeers' enormous brains and even more enormous tea intake, no one quite believed that this would work. And if it didn't, there was no second chance. The amazing thing was, it did work. In fact, it worked brilliantly. So well that no one cared that the car didn't beat the skiing man. For once, *Top Gear* had set out to do something and not made an utter cock of it. The little Mini became a part of the studio set and its fire-spitting run was immortalised in the *Top Gear* title sequence. After its heroic flight, it had more than earned it.

PEEL P50

Series 10, episode 3

First transmitted: 28 October 2007

Filming locations:
Holland Park and Shepherds Bush, London;
BBC White City and BBC Television Centre, London.

JEREMY became obsessed with the microscopic Peel P50 after seeing one in a car museum and was itching for the chance to get it on *Top Gear*. That chance came in 2007 when he used one to get – quite literally – into the office. That was the actual *Top Gear* office featured in the item, though the team has now moved to a different office where there's less chance of John Humphrys coming in and 'borrowing' things.

The other offices were real BBC departments too, with equally real reactions from the staff who had

no idea that the silly man from *Top Gear* was about to come charging through in a tiny car, hastily followed by a film crew. The only sop to filming inside was an extra filter on the exhaust to prevent the fumes from choking everyone while they sat at their desk.

Some years later, the team were working on a follow-up involving a journey across New York City with a route that potentially encompassed office buildings, shops and the *Sesame Street* set. The plan was eventually aborted because, in truth, it could never beat the brilliant, hilarious simplicity of the original.

HAMMERHEAD-i EAGLE THRUST

Series 14, episode 2

First transmitted: 22 November 2009

Filming locations:
The Top Gear Technology Centre, Didcot, Oxfordshire;
Oxford, Oxfordshire;
the top secret MIRA test facility; Teddington, Middlesex.

IT was Jeremy who first wondered if *Top Gear* could build an electric car that was both cheaper and better than a G-Wiz. He almost certainly suffixed the suggestion with the words, 'How hard can it be?' To suss out the competition, one of the programme's producers went undercover to an electric-car show at the Millbrook proving ground where he was swiftly outed as a member of the *Top Gear* team and treated with a winning combination of suspicion and contempt. Nonetheless, he quickly established that the current crop of electric cars wasn't very good and building something better should be a piece of cake. Hammond was put in charge of sourcing something

with a separate chassis upon which the TG electro-car could be based. His shortlist consisted of a Land Rover (which would have been too big and too heavy), a Lincoln Town Car (ditto, and hard to get hold of in the UK) or an old TVR. He plumped for the latter, and the TG Technology Centre's tame mechanic used his contacts in the TVR world to

find a shabby Chimaera with a battered body and a ruined interior but – crucially – a sound chassis. Meanwhile, Jeremy came up with an innovative way of making a body, using the frames from modular shelving units and sheets of aluminium. Off-camera he experimented with even lighter panelling made from the thick plastic used for estate agent's signs

but it was too flimsy. Aluminium offered the right blend of lightness and strength, and who cared that it was dangerously reflective in bright sunlight and left lethally sharp edges all over the place? Only the doors were made from wood (with 'locks' provided by the sliding bolts from a garden shed) after aluminium proved too floppy.

Hammond's chassis mated to Clarkson's body made for a remarkably light car. Unfortunately, this was almost immediately offset by the installation of May's motor-and-battery combo, which weighed more than the moon and lacked the power or the range to be of any use. This was all too graphically proven when the TG volt machine brought bedlam

to the centre of Oxford, earning the presenters some stern words from a policeman, and then whirred into the countryside, ran out of electricity and careered into a tree.

A second-generation version of the car was far more dynamic, starting with the name, which was changed from 'Geoff' to 'Hammerhead-i Eagle Thrust'. More importantly, the new model now featured detail improvements including an impact-absorbing front bumper (a steel bar on two old coil springs), low-rolling resistance wheels (TVR space-saver spares fitted with Citroen 2CV tyres), and an ingenious on-board power station (a second-hand diesel generator acquired from a race

team who, it later turned out, had been banned from using it in the pit lane because it was too noisy and smelly).

Confident that they had created a winner, the presenters headed to the MIRA proving ground where even the on-site engineers and test drivers – people used to seeing top secret prototypes and outlandish test mules from Lamborghini, Bugatti, Jaguar, et al – stopped what they were doing to watch with gaping disbelief as the Thrusthammer Eaglehead-i demonstrated its excellence (or something similar).

The presenters were pretty pleased with the way the Eaglehammer performed, the death of Eco Stig

notwithstanding, and the production team were genuinely staggered at the way the car stood up to the cobbled test track, the wind tunnel and the drag strip without faltering. What wasn't shown on the programme was the rigorous government inspection the car had to undergo when it rolled out of the TG Tech Centre for the first time. To everyone's amazement, it actually passed without a problem and was immediately declared fully road-legal. It really was a proper, working car. Yet strangely, no one has ever contacted the office to ask if they could buy a Thrusteagle i-Headhammer of their own. Jeremy, Richard and James still blame that harsh review in *Autocar*.

THE CONVERTIBLE PEOPLE CARRIER

Series 8, episode 1

First transmitted: 7 May 2006

Filming locations: High Wycombe, Buckinghamshire;
Millbrook Proving Ground, Bedfordshire;
Woburn Safari Park, Bedfordshire; Bedford, Bedfordshire.

YOU can buy a convertible version of almost any sort of car, yet no one has ever built a soft-top people carrier. Jeremy, Richard and James decided to make amends. Their starting point was a Renault Espace, which, uniquely in the people-carrier world, has a separate chassis and a non-structural body, so that slicing the roof off shouldn't cause it to fall apart, as it would with most cars. And amazingly, this theory proved correct.

Then came the really tricky bit – making a hood. Proper car companies spend millions on this, often sub-contracting the work to companies that are devoted solely to designing sturdy, waterproof, draught-free roofs that retract in seconds at the touch of a button. The presenters didn't have millions of pounds nor access to any dedicated roof-design companies. They had some canvas, some metal tubes and James May's blackboard. It was never going to end well.

Whilst Clarkson, Hammond and May got on with beheading their Espace, the *Top Gear* production team plotted a series of tests for the finished

As well as featuring the convertible people carrier, the first programme of series eight also introduced a furry fourth presenter who was added to the team after a big pre-series ideas meeting where James May, upon being asked if he had anything to add, looked up from his notebook and said, 'Could we get a dog?' Top Gear Dog stopped featuring on the show because she was basically useless and didn't do anything. She still lives with Hammond and his family.

product. Millbrook Proving Ground was chosen for track testing, mainly for its high-speed bowl but also for its proximity to Woburn Safari Park and, in particular, its monkey enclosure. Around this time the production team were inexplicably obsessed with monkeys. There had even been some slightly deranged scheme to see if a monkey could drive an automatic car, a plan that was very rapidly kyboshed by an expert at a well-known simian sanctuary who had threatened to 'shut down' the entire programme if such an endeavour was ever attempted. Unbowed,

the TG office seized on a new way to get monkeys on the show, by forcing the presenters to drive their decapitated Espace through the Barbary ape compound at Woburn. It worked rather well, especially after the producers threw food onto the flimsy canvas roof, prompting an immortal Hammond yell: 'Attack monkey!'

In the end, the convertible people carrier survived the apes but was outfaced by a simple car wash. Maybe that's why, to date, no carmaker has attempted to build a convertible model of their own.

REASONABLY PRICED CAR 2 THE CHEVROLET LACETTI

Series 8–14

First transmitted: 2006

AFTER seven series of new *Top Gear*, the celebrity lap-board was getting rather full. There was talk of building a taller board, or one with two columns, but neither seemed a very practical answer to the problem. Plus, Suzuki had stopped selling the Liana and a car couldn't really be called reasonably priced if it was impossible to buy one.

The only answer was to find a new Reasonably Priced Car. It's sometimes asked why the star guests don't get to set their lap times in something more exciting and powerful. The truth is, even if *Top Gear* could get hold of a Lamborghini Gallardo or a Porsche 911 Turbo every week and find the budget to replace clutches, brakes and all the other things that take a hammering on the track, our celebrities are a mixed bag of abilities and it wouldn't be a good idea to give them something in which they could hit 170mph, panic and plough wildly into a field / jumbo jet / cameraman. The liability insurance for putting valuable stars in such jeopardy would be insanely high. Plus, a small, front-wheel-drive hatchback is a great leveller. Those who know what they're doing extract every last drop of performance and grip – just watch the F1 drivers in the Liana for example – and those who don't aren't

in danger of cartwheeling down the runway in a horrible fireball.

So there was no question of replacing the Liana with anything other than another dull, low-powered saloon. And it had to be reasonably priced. The segment would have to be renamed if it wasn't. The Lacetti fitted the bill perfectly and Chevrolet provided a brand new example, standard apart from a roll cage and a race seat, plus an identical back-up in case something went wrong with the lead car. The Lacetti went on to pound the track for seven series but it never quite wormed its way into the *Top Gear* team's affections like the Liana. Where the little Suzuki grew to look endearingly gawky, the Chevy just looked boring and, though it was a faster car, it wasn't especially enjoyable to lap, not least because it was blighted by a clunky and obstructive gear change. Watch how many Lacetti-driving celebrities cursed a missed gear to see that problem writ large.

It was a dependable track servant but the Chevy was never really loved. Which is probably why Hammond was able to mark the end of its time as the Reasonably Priced Car by exploding an industrial chimney on top of it. And nobody really cared.

CLASSIC ROAD RALLY CARS

Series 13, episode 6
First transmitted: 26 July 2009
Filming locations:
King's Lynn, Norfolk; most of Majorca.

MANY people have claimed that old cars are more fun and more interesting than new ones. Richard and James weren't sure about this. Jeremy very definitely wasn't sure about this. In fact, he openly thought it was nonsense. And that gave *Top Gear*'s producers a cheeky idea; force the presenters to buy an old car each at auction and then make them enter a complicated time trial rally with it. It's fair to say that Hammond, May and Clarkson weren't entirely keen on this idea. They were even less keen when they discovered that the auction they'd be attending was in King's Lynn, which is miles from where any of them lives and takes an age to get to. Actually, this regular King's Lynn auction is well known in classic car circles for reasons that aren't entirely clear, except that over

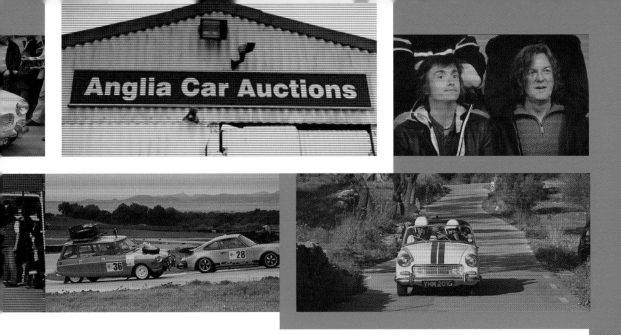

the road from the auction house there's an enormous pornography shop. It's more of a warehouse really. But this is almost certainly an entirely unrelated issue. The auction process actually went quite smoothly and all three presenters ended up with cars. Jeremy's Austin-Healey actually seemed quite good. Considering that it was a last-minute panic purchase, James's wasn't bad either. Even Richard's Lanchester was fixable. Somehow, the reluctant trio had done well. The programme's producers were slightly annoyed by this. What they'd inadvertently done was let them buy perfectly reasonable old cars and now they were going to send them off to a sunny island in the Mediterranean where they'd probably have a perfectly nice time tootling about in the sunshine. There was only one thing for it – make mischief.

First of all, they sent the presenters out late so they were always going to be playing catch-up and doing ludicrously complicated maths in the time trials. And second of all, they arranged for the presenters to be accompanied by wholly unhelpful co-drivers. Jeremy's was incomprehensible, Richard's was incapable of seeing over the dashboard, James's was pneumatically disinterested in cars, driving or

regularity time trial rallying. Everyone in the office was cruelly delighted with this wheeze at the time. Despite the *Top Gear* team's best efforts to make the presenters' lives miserable, this was one of *Top Gear*'s less arduous shoots. Yes, Hammond's Lanchester overheated literally every 10 minutes, and yes, the whole crew spent their trip fending off perma-sozzled British ex-pats, but otherwise it was

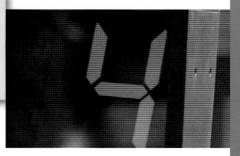

a welcome reminder that actually old cars are okay, even if – as Richard discovered with dismay back in Britain – it turns out that your grandfather didn't make them.

There's a happy ending to this tale too because Jeremy and James became so attached to their cars that both bought them off the producers once the rally was over. Actually, Jeremy already had £600 of his own money tied up in his Sprite, but that's not the point. He really, really loved that car and wanted his daughter to learn to drive in it whilst James was equally attached to his Citroen and imagined that his girlfriend might enjoy driving it around London. Strangely, both were mistaken and the two cars are now on permanent loan to the car museum where Richard's wretched Lanchester lives.

THE BOTSWANA SPECIAL

Series 10, episode 4

First transmitted: 4 November 2007

Filming locations:
The Botswana / Zimbabwe border;
the Makgadikgadi pan;
the Okavango Delta;
the Botswana / Namibia border.

JEREMY had recently enjoyed a holiday in Botswana and came into the *Top Gear* office raving about the majesty and variety of its terrain. It would be, he reckoned, the perfect place to shoot the next hour-long special.

The producers liked the idea. Plainly, however, they couldn't send Clarkson, Hammond and May off on a nice holiday. This would have to be made challenging and interesting for them. A central challenge was hatched, based around demonstrating that you don't need a big, heavy, high-riding 4x4. Our boys would prove this by crossing the very spine of Africa in ordinary, two-wheel-drive cars.

Having been given this brief, the presenters hastened to the internet where they quickly discovered that Botswanian *Auto Trader* is as bleak and featureless as the Makgadikgadi salt pan. It also contains about as many cars. Their search widened to nearby South Africa and it was here that Jeremy made one of the daftest decisions of his life. His car for this hot, lengthy and unquestionably arduous journey would be a Lancia Beta Coupé. The Beta in question, the only one for sale in the whole of Africa it seemed, had been on the market for over a year and even the chap selling it couldn't quite believe that someone wanted to take it off his hands. Little wonder, because it was quite simply a total mutt.

Even before they'd laid eyes on it, the producers heard the word 'Lancia' and immediately assumed that Jeremy wouldn't make it to the end of the journey. If he conked out halfway through – or, as seemed more likely in an ancient Beta Coupé, 500 yards from the start – what would he do? Passenger one of the other presenters? Jump on the next plane home? Then someone had a brilliant idea: introduce a forfeit car. And to make sure it really was a forfeit, the car in question had to be one that all three presenters despise – the Volkswagen Beetle.

Not that it seemed James would need it, because he'd been more sensible in his car choice and picked up an old Mercedes 230 taxi that, judging from the massive mileage, had spent its time ferrying people back and forth to the moon. Richard, like Jeremy, had been less rational. He simply saw a picture of an Opel Kadett for sale and decided that was the car he wanted.

On the epic journey between the Zimbabwean and Namibian borders, the cars performed pretty much as you would expect. James's Mercedes ran almost flawlessly and was so well bolted together that it

took twice as long as Jeremy's Lancia to strip off its panels at the edge of the salt flats. Richard's Opel had the odd glitch, mostly related to inadvisable immersion in water, but was otherwise remarkably stout. And, unsurprisingly, Jeremy's Lancia was a complete disaster that teetered constantly on the verge of total mechanical failure, enormous electrical meltdown and spontaneous engine-bay fire. There were several moments when it looked like Clarkson really would end up in the Beetle, yet every time the knackered Beta would somehow spring back into life at the last minute.

Incredibly, the Lancia made it to the finish point but it was failing with such tedious regularity that some of the breakdowns had to be cut out of the final edit to save time. Also squeezed from the finished programme were Jeremy's bush mechanic master class in which he (badly) made a driveshaft out of wood, and an ill-fated attempt to cross the river using a local technique whereby the car is wrapped in a tarpaulin that is then inflated with air so that it can be floated across the river. This turned out to be far more complicated than the presenters imagined and after three-and-a-half

TOP FACT

Speaking on Chris Evans's Radio 2 show in March 2012, Jeremy declared the Botswana special to be his favourite thing Top Gear has ever done.

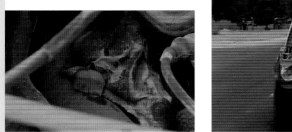

hours of inept flailing about, the whole idea was abandoned.

Something else that didn't appear in the show was the moment when a local guide discovered that Jeremy and Richard had put raw meat and a cow's head in James's car and gave them the most almighty telling off for putting the whole crew at risk from animal attack. There was a lot of mumbling and looking at shoes after that one.

Fortunately, no one got savaged by a lion. Nor did anyone get bitten by crocodiles, attacked by hippos or have their gentleman's area savaged by a honey

badger. All in all, the trip was a great success. This was especially true for Richard, who fell in love with Oliver the Opel and, after filming was completed, had him shipped back to the UK where they live together to this day. The Mercedes was given to a local man who had advised the team on filming in Botswana and the wretched Beetle, grudgingly declared the most dependable car there, was donated to the bush mechanic who had helped to keep the other cars running.

As for the Lancia, well that was just scrap. But then frankly, it was just scrap when Jeremy bought it.

TOYOTA AYGO CAR FOOTBALL

Series 6, episode 1
First transmitted: 22 May 2005
Filming location: Bruntingthorpe Proving Ground, Leicestershire.

A man from Toyota got in touch with *Top Gear* and said he had a bunch of brand new Aygos and a burning desire to see if you could play football with them. The only problem was, since no one had tried this before, it was impossible to say if you really could hold a soccer match using cars. The only thing for it was to get the Aygos wrapped in team colours, have a bouncy-castle manufacturer create a batch of massive footballs, find a suitably large area to act as a pitch and give it a go. To everyone's amazement, car football didn't just work; it worked brilliantly. At first, Hammond, May and their team-mates played with polite delicacy. But once it became clear that an actual game was possible, everyone's competitive streak began to emerge. Even James May's. This would have meant little more than a gentle upping of the pace, but for the presence of one thing – touring-car drivers. These are chaps who aren't afraid of a little coming-together and as the match progressed the contact got more regular and more aggressive. Standing on the sidelines, the man from Toyota described it as like a cross between 'a sport and a motorway pile up'. It was a good job they'd disabled the airbags. Yet the little cars stood up to this punishment and to subsequent 'matches' including a twice-a-day pounding during the *Top Gear Live* shows and another televised battering against a team of small Volkswagens during series eight.

Top Gear has played sports with other cars since, but nothing seems able to resist the crash and bash of a competitive game like the little Aygo. Eventually, Toyota took the original hard worn batch of ten 'players' (plus two substitutes) and, to prevent them ending up on eBay, dispatched them to the scrapyard. A shame, yes, but you had to say the lads done good, Brian.

TOP FACT

Toyota recently told Top Gear that when the engineering team responsible for the next Aygo first met up they inspired themselves to get cracking by playing a DVD of the original car football film.

THE POLAR SPECIAL HILUX

Series 9, episode 7

First transmitted: 25 July 2007

Filming locations: Resolute, Canada; the Arctic; the magnetic North Pole (1996 location).

THE race to the North Pole was one of the most difficult and dangerous things *Top Gear* has ever attempted. Not that the presenters realised this when they spent most of their Arctic survival training course mucking about, received a proper telling-off and were forced to do it all again. Even after that, it took a few stern words from legendary explorer Sir Ranulph Fiennes before they truly realised just what lay ahead.

Fortunately, the production team were taking things more seriously and knew there was only one vehicle suitable for the task in hand – the indestructible Toyota Hilux. In fact, two Hiluxes were acquired from Toyota – both bright red to stand out in the relentlessly white landscape – and both were dispatched to Iceland, where the boffins at a company called Arctic Trucks set about making them suitable for the epic journey ahead. The suspension

was beefed up and dropped down and forward from the bodywork to allow space for the massive 38-inch wheels, the differentials were switched for stronger units capable of 100 per cent locking, fuel and coolant heaters were added to allow the engines to work reliably in sub-zero conditions, stronger batteries were installed, heavy-duty skid plates were bolted to the undersides, and bigger fuel tanks were fitted to allow greater range. Even the diesel within them was of a unique freeze-resistant formula. Jeremy and James drove one truck, the film crew had the other, and the Icelanders came along to provide technical support in their similarly modified Toyota Land Cruiser.

No such luxury for Richard Hammond, whose only back-up was a film crew and a medic travelling on skidoos. Worse yet, he had to travel to the far north of Canada a whole week before James and Jeremy

in order to receive dog-sled training. And on the journey itself, he rapidly discovered that his travelling options were either skiing, which was physically punishing, or standing on the sled, in which case he would be intermittently sprayed with dog poo. With this in mind, Hammond's misery was often clear to viewers. Making Jeremy's and James's

most uncomfortable moments come across on TV wasn't easy because sheer cold doesn't really show up on screen. However, if you look at their craggy, bleary-eyed, unshaven faces towards the end of the programme you'll quickly gather that it wasn't an effortless whirl of brisk driving and sloe gin. Although if you asked James to name the worst part of this

expedition, he'd instantly say, 'Sharing a tent with Jeremy.' Jeremy's worst moment would be 'Sharing a tent with James'.

The race was, of course, won by the Hilux, which thereby became the first car ever to reach the magnetic North Pole. Jeremy and James weren't going to sit around waiting for Richard at the finish and, via a distinctly patchy communications system, the toughest and bravest *Top Gear* presenter on the ice was told to abort his mission. He never made it to the pole and instead diverted to a specially carved landing strip where all three presenters were extracted by plane and taken back to somewhere warmer.

THE MID-ENGINED SUPERCARS FOR £10,000 CHALLENGE

Series 7, episode 4

First transmitted: 4 December 2005

Filming locations: Great Western Dockyard, Bristol;
Castle Combe circuit, Wiltshire;
Chippenham, Wiltshire; Marlborough, Wiltshire;
Reading, Berkshire; just outside Slough, Berkshire.

TOP GEAR had bought cars for £100 or less (which had proved surprisingly successful); *Top Gear* had bought Porsches for £1,500 or less (which had proved that you shouldn't get a 928 unless you want to turn it into furniture); *Top Gear* had bought £1,500 coupés that weren't Porsches (which had proved that grass racing is fun but you'd probably still want a Porsche). Now it was time to go for the big one – supercars.

Clearly, a budget of £1,500 wasn't going to cut it. After all, these are fine Italian thoroughbreds we're talking about here, and even the shabbiest example still has value. But could you get one for about the price of a two-year-old Ford Mondeo?

Finding suitable cars wasn't the work of a moment

but with a concerted trawl through the classic car mags and the oilier corners of the internet, the presenters managed it. Keen students of the supercar will note that one thing the presenters' cars – the Maserati Merak, the Lamborghini Urraco and the Dino 308 GT4 – had in common was that, unusually for mid-engined cars, they all had back seats. And supercars with back seats are traditionally not popular, hence their slide into sub-£10,000 territory.

However, as a day's worth of challenges quickly proved, the other reason these cars were so relatively affordable was because they were basically knackered. Jeremy's Maser, for example, may have boasted a rebuilt engine but it was clear that it had been rebuilt badly. It was also claimed

to be the rare and desirable Merak SS, when in fact the only part on it from an actual Merak SS was the SS badge. You would think that its mechanical problems would only worsen when Jeremy was instructed to change the oil and the spark plugs. After all, whilst Hammond and May know their way around an engine and are never happier than when they're getting their hands dirty, Clarkson is wilfully spanner-phobic. So it was a shock to find that, actually, he does know the basic principles of where spark plugs live and even beat James in the supercar servicing challenge.

May lost the parking test too, though this might have been because the production team had reserved spaces using BBC hire cars, thereby giving a giggling Clarkson and Hammond access to their keys and

TOP FACT

Jeremy and James were happy to see their supercars sold to specialist garages who intended to break them down for parts. Richard, however, became rather attached to his 308 and bought it off the programme.

allowing them to move one of the cars until the space was plainly too small for May's malfunctioning Lambo. Or rather, it was plainly too small to everyone in the ever-growing crowd but not, as it turns out, to Captain Spatial Awareness.

Despite their obvious failings, it seemed absurd to think that these three supercars couldn't even make the 100-odd-mile journey from Bristol to Slough. Yet,

depressingly, they couldn't. Clarkson's entire bottom end exploded. Hammond's engine electrical system shut down. And, once again, James May ran out of electricity.

Back in the studio, all scoring was rendered null and void because this challenge left only one, glaringly obvious conclusion. Yes, you can buy a supercar for less than £10,000. But for the love of God, don't.

THE AMERICA SPECIAL

Series 9, episode 3

First transmitted: 11 February 2007

Filming locations: Miami Dade;
Moroso Motor Sports Park, Florida;
Seminole, Alabama;
New Orleans, Louisiana.

THE America special was never intended to be an hour-long epic nor a programme in its own right. Yet inadvertently it set the template for *Top Gear* specials and foreign road trips that endures to this day.

The idea of doing a long journey in the United States had been discussed in the production office many times and the basic premise – can you do it in a car that cost less than it would cost you to hire one? – was considered strong enough to make a substantial two-part film for a normal programme in series nine. It was only when the team returned from America that they realised there was simply too much good stuff to cram into 25 or 30 minutes of TV and a whole show was devoted to Jeremy, Richard and James making their way from Miami to New Orleans. It was fitting that their endeavours were given a full hour of television since this was, up to that point, one of the most arduous and intensive shoots *Top Gear* had ever undertaken – starting with a

struggle to find the cars themselves. In order to make the premise of the whole trip stand up, the presenters had just $1,000 each and that, as it turned out, was not a lot in the Floridian used-car market. It was made worse because James was in full Captain Comfort mode and desperately wanted a Cadillac, even though such things were rare within budget. Meanwhile, Jeremy was after some sort of laughable jock rocket and couldn't help being drawn to various unsavoury Camaros and Trans Ams,

almost all of which were little more than heaps of rust held together with the blood of murdered hitchhikers. It seemed inevitable that Hammond would end up either with a Jeep or a pick-up truck but those too were largely out of his price range. It was starting to look hopeless.

There was a very real worry that the presenters would end up with no cars at all, but with perseverance they came through and headed to an agreed meeting point to compare notes and begin

their journey. Unfortunately, as Hammond drove to the rendezvous point in his newly acquired pick-up, he spotted an older, cooler, more battered truck that he liked the look of even more. After some frantic bartering with the owner – and some even more frantic bartering with one of the producers, who agreed to release more funds if the first truck could be returned – a deal was done. Hammond was delighted and his grin didn't fade until at least a mile down the road when his new truck broke

down. There were more frantic conversations leading to some quite ugly arguments and the original pick-up was hastily brought back into play. From Miami, the presenters and their shabby, sub-$1,000 cars rumbled up the highway bringing confusion and chaos to the good people of the southeastern United States. At the Moroso Raceway, their late braking and perilously close calls with alligator-infested swamps caused the panicked circuit organisers to deploy their emergency response

unit. Which turned out to be a man in a golf cart. At one hotel, the mere sight of Clarkson's manky Camaro the next morning caused the manager to inform Jeremy that he would not be welcome at this establishment again. And then there was the infamous cow-on-the roof incident. That caused quite a stink when the programme was transmitted, but not as much as the stink it caused to Jeremy's actual car as it gently leaked foul-smelling cow juice into the interior and caused such a funk that the entire passenger seat and much of the interior trim had to be removed from the car and thrown away. As the BBC was forced to explain at the time, the cow had died of natural causes and had been lying in a field in the fetid heat and humidity of a Florida summer for several days. As a result, it was very far from fresh. Very, very far from fresh.

The cow, however, wasn't the most memorable moment in the American road trip. That would be the ill-fated Alabama slogan challenge. This was an idea

TOP FACT

The car lot selling ex-police cars that was seen in this programme proudly boasted of supplying many of the cop cruisers wrecked in the movie Bad Boys II.

that had been mulled over by the *Top Gear* production team for some time, originally as something called the Texas Smart Car Challenge, in which someone would see how far across the Lone Star state they could drive in a bright pink Smart with 'Man-Love Rules OK' written on the side. It was hard to justify sending a presenter all the way to America just to get embarrassed and very possibly beaten up, but when the US road trip came along it seemed the perfect time to dust off the basic idea. Out in the field, each presenter was given some paint and a bit of paper with some suggested ideas for inflammatory things to write on their colleagues' cars. And, in truth, the producers had no idea if this challenge would yield anything interesting. *Top Gear* has since tried the slogan trick in other places, such as Bolivia, and it's elicited very little reaction. But in Alabama, it went way beyond what anyone could have expected.

Top Gear has since been asked if the scary scene in the gas station that looked poised to turn into

a lynching was somehow set up. The answer is 'No'. Those were real people and they were real angry. It was all rather frightening, not least for the last film crew left on the forecourt, who had been riding with executive producer Andy Wilman in their back seat and returned to their car only to find him gone. On the basis that you never leave a man behind, they waited as disgruntled hicks circled the car only to finally make phone contact and discover that, in the panic, Wilman had leapt into the wrong crew car and was now safely some three or four miles up the road.

It was quite a trip and one that drove the entire team to the brink of exhaustion. On top of this, nothing prepared them for the shocking devastation that Hurricane Katrina had wreaked upon New Orleans. In the face of such a sobering sight, it was only right that the presenters abandoned all thought of selling their cars and gave them away instead.

REASONABLY PRICED CAR 3 THE KIA CEE'D

Series 15–present

First transmitted: 2010

JUST as the Chevrolet Lacetti was coming to the end of its time as the Reasonably Priced Car, the *Top Gear* office received what James May would call GOOD NEWS! The Dacia Sandero was going on sale in Britain and its makers were offering it as our next celebrity track hack. This was perfect. Thanks to May's weird obsession with it, the Sandero was already well known to TG viewers, it looked nerdishly amusing, and though UK prices were yet to be confirmed, they were guaranteed to be well within the ballpark of reasonable. The company behind it, Renault, even took one of the production team to a secret location in west London to have a look at the only Sandero in the UK and made bold promises that, if *Top Gear* was still interested, the roll cage and race seat would be fitted by the boffins who ran the Clio Cup race series so they'd be of the highest quality. Everyone was very excited.

But then... BAD NEWS! The economy tanked, Renault flinched at the cost of launching Dacia in the UK and plans to bring the Sandero to Britain were cancelled. *Top Gear* would have to find something else to be the next Reasonably Priced Car. Question was, what? Since new *Top Gear* started back in 2002 it seemed that fewer and fewer carmakers offered things that could genuinely be called reasonably priced. Perhaps it was time for a change. A few alternative options were bandied around the office including the Mazda MX5, which would, if nothing else, bring a rear-wheel-drive chassis and therefore the prospect of some lurid drifting, especially in the wet. On the downside, its tiny interior made it difficult to package the minicams to film the celebrities' faces and equipping it with a sturdy roll cage may have necessitated leaving the soft top down permanently, even in the depths of winter. No, what was needed was just another normal, un-sporty, front-wheel-drive saloon or hatchback and the Kia Cee'd fitted the bill perfectly. It was well-priced, it was well-made and, having experienced them as hire cars whilst on film shoots, the TG team knew it was actually rather nice to drive. Happily, Kia agreed to supply two identical cars plus an automatic version that later had to be modified for track work because its computer simply couldn't comprehend someone using full throttle for that amount of time.

Thus far, the Cee'd has done well. It's proven dependable, quick, and its retro-fitted race seat has accommodated a glittering array of celebrity bottoms including Tom Cruise, Cameron Diaz, Matt LeBlanc, Ryan Reynolds and, erm, John Prescott. In fact, about the only thing wrong with it is that bloody stupid apostrophe in its name.

RELIANT ROBIN SPACE SHUTTLE

Series 9, episode 4

First transmitted: 18 February 2007

Filming locations: Glossop, Derbyshire;
Avon Model Aeroplane Club;
University of the West of England, Bristol;
Otterburn Artillery Range, Northumberland.

JEREMY Clarkson likes to claim that he hasn't been wrong about anything since 1974. And he was pretty confident that this situation wasn't about to change when he declared Hammond and May's cut-price space shuttle plan to be stupid and guaranteed to fail.

Still, nothing spurs James and Richard on like the prospect of putting some egg on Clarkson's face. The Reliant-based rocket was a good idea, and it was going to work. But the project wasn't without setbacks. First problem – the Reliant that Hammond bought conked out before he'd had a chance to film it driving around Derbyshire. Happily, of all the places they could have been shooting, they just happened to be mere minutes away from a place called World Of Reliants. Or something like that. A new Robin was bought for a song and they were away. Now there was just the small matter of building a rocket powerful enough to get the silly

little car into the air. And the *Top Gear* duo knew they were in safe hands because they were calling on the skills of the same Rocket Men who'd made a Mini fly down a ski-jump. With brains the size of the moon and an appetite for tea the size of Jupiter, these boys would get the job done. Although, in truth, even they were a bit phased by the size of the task in hand. Still, they dealt with it the only way they knew how – put the kettle on and do a few calculations on the back of a laptop. They soon worked out that, even with the Reliant stripped of as much weight as possible – an intensive process that extended to details like new, lighter wheels – they would require a massive eight-and-a-half tons of thrust to get it off the ground. And that takes some doing.

It's easy to watch something on telly and assume that just because it looks simple, it actually is. But this project really did push the boundaries of what could be achieved by a semi-pro team of enthusiastic

rocket-ists. In fact, for a meagre budget and to a punishing schedule, what they would have to build was the largest and most powerful non-commercial rocket ever constructed in Europe. And they were doing it in Glossop. From a shed.

Richard and James knew the Rocketeers wouldn't let them down – and they didn't. The finished Robin-and-rockets combo looked magnificent when it was assembled at the launch site in the northeast of England. All those late nights, all that head scratching,

all those millions of gallons of tea, it all started to seem worth it.

Which makes what happened next all the more heartbreaking. The launch had already been delayed for the very un-NASA-like reason that a rogue cow had trampled over some of the cabling that linked the launch pad to the mission control bunker. But with all the computers talking to each other once more, the countdown was on. And as it clicked the zero, the absurd shuttle and its mighty propulsion

system fired majestically into the Northumbrian sky, exactly as planned. At 1,000 feet, the two solid rocket boosters detached and drifted slowly earthwards on parachutes, also exactly as planned. But then... disaster. One of the explosive bolts that should have fired to detach the orbiter from the main fuel tank simply didn't go off and, instead of soaring free into the atmosphere and then swooping down to the landing strip, the little Robin was stuck to a dead weight that pulled it inexorably into the ground.

The expressions on the faces of the rocket men said it all. They really thought this was going to work. They'd put in a mind-boggling amount of effort to make damn sure that it would. And now all that hard work had come crashing back down to earth. They were inconsolable.

Only one thing was worse than trying to cheer up a gaggle of gutted Northerners – seeing Jeremy's smug face when he found out that Hammond and May's ingenious budget shuttle plan had failed.

THE BRITISH LEYLAND CHALLENGE

Series 10, episode 7

First transmitted: 25 November 2007

Filming locations: Warwick Services, Warwickshire;
Cowley, Oxfordshire; Canley, Coventry; Longbridge, Birmingham;
the top secret MIRA test facility, Watling Street, Nuneaton, Warwickshire;
CVIO OTU (on the A5, between Hinkley and Atherstone, just before the A444.
If you get to Fenny Drayton you've gone too far);
the Top Gear test track, Surrey.

THIS challenge came about after a furious debate over British Leyland and whether the defunct car giant had ever done anything worthwhile. The presenters backed themselves into an argument-based dead end on this one, the only way out of which was to buy some bloody BL cars and make an item about it. Also, it was 39 years since BL's formation and, in the rounding-up world of *Top Gear* maths, that made it an anniversary, too.

Having bought their cars, Jeremy, Richard and James were told to meet at Warwick Services on the M40 and, on the assumption that they wouldn't make the rendezvous with the proper film crew, each was given a mini video camera so they could record the moment when they broke down. Yet amazingly, all three presenters made it from their homes to the start point. It was when they left Warwick that the problems started, as Hammond's Dolomite Sprint conked out just 100

yards down the road, still on the slip road out of the service station.

At the head of the pack, James was unaware of this problem and carried merrily on his way until a walkie-talkie message told him to pull off at the next exit to wait for his colleagues. Led by the film crew in a Range Rover tracking car, he did just that. Unfortunately, the exit they took was for Gaydon, which is where Land Rover has its headquarters. As a result, there are a lot of other Range Rovers on the roads in this area and, displaying the sense of directional awareness for which he is famed, James inadvertently latched onto the wrong dark blue Range Rover and followed it for several miles across Warwickshire, blissfully failing to notice that its tailgate wasn't open and it didn't have a ruddy great TV camera poking out of the back.

Things didn't get much better when the trio reunited, as their attempts to find BL's remains turned into a depressing reminder of how the

company's empire had been sold or demolished. The presenters ended up on the levelled ground where part of Austin's vast Longbridge plant once stood, and came up with an improvised musical piece based on the various squeaks and clunks made by their cars. Even this, and an unusually bright, sunny day, couldn't stop it being a rather depressing place to be.

The rattling, parping presenters and their rattling, parping cars moved on to the MIRA test track in Warwickshire. *Top Gear* regularly makes a gag out of the secret nature of these places but it's no joke and the staff at all industry proving grounds are very sensitive about filming there, constantly reminding you not to point cameras at any of the other cars on site, lest they be something that hasn't yet been made public. They also, as it turns out, don't like it when three idiots leave bits of old car all over their Belgian pavé facility and allow a runaway Triumph Dolomite to clatter into one of

their signs. Shortly afterwards, *Top Gear* made its excuses and left.

In the planning of this item, the production team had struggled to come up with a dramatic final test, until someone had the bright idea of filling the cars with water, exposing poor manufacturing and poor performance in one go. The cars were taken briefly from the presenters so that filling and breathing holes could be cut in the roof and the ignition electrics could be re-sited.

BL enthusiasts weren't happy about this rather destructive test, but the truth is the cars that the presenters bought were very far from the finest examples of the breed and, by way of some small compensation, the Rover and the Princess survive to this day in a museum.

Better yet, the Dolomite was donated to *Top Gear*'s tame mechanic Steve and, inspired by 1970s touring cars, he has been (slowly) turning it into a retro track day car.

THE £1,500 PORSCHE CHALLENGE

Series 5, episode 6

First transmitted: 5 December 2004

Filming locations: Exchange Square, London;
Brighton, East Sussex;
the Top Gear test track, Surrey.

SPURRED on by the surprise success of the £100 challenge in series 4, the producers decided to think bigger. Many, many people dream of owning a Porsche, but could you do so for a minimal amount of money? Clearly, £100 would be too low, but five minutes scouting around the darkest recesses of the internet seemed to suggest that £1,500 would be a reasonable target. As it turned out, Hammond secured a Porsche for just half of that amount. Admittedly, it was a 924 with, as James and Jeremy kept pointing out, 'a van engine', but it had a Porsche badge on the front nonetheless. May also

managed to come in well under budget with his 944 for £900, but Clarkson, typically, had been rather more ambitious. And rubbish. Clearly he'd never buy a 911 because he hates them, and anyway they never become especially cheap unless they've been through a hedge backwards. No, Jeremy had gone further than that by spending every penny of his £1,500 budget on the most complicated Porsche he could find – the V8-engined 928. Little wonder that the first challenge, a simple 55-mile drive from London to Brighton, took an entire day and resulted in Jeremy arriving at the coast on the back of an AA lorry. Things didn't get much better at the track,

where The Stig discovered that the worn suspension bushes and ageing tyres on the 944 and 928 led to some distinctly interesting handling characteristics. The men from the Porsche Club of Great Britain showed no mercy in their detailed evaluation of the vehicles' originality and condition, which was scarce and terrible respectively.

Things were especially bad for Jeremy since his V8 Porsche was now running on just six-and-a-bit cylinders and spewing out all manner of odd-smelling fluids and gases. It was also covered in badly applied blackboard paint. However, in the final reckoning he drew inspiration from the very chairs used on the *Top*

Gear set and a company that had sent a press release to the *Top Gear* office some weeks earlier advertising a range of coffee tables made from old engine blocks. By dismembering his sickly 928 he made a slightly kitsch living room set and flogged it for a profit to win the challenge.

There is, however, a happy ending for Hammond's 924 because, whilst he failed to sell it at the end of the programme, it was eventually bought by one of the production team's relatives who, to this day, happily uses it to compete in time trials and autocross events. It still has the flames on the side.

AMPHIBIOUS CARS 2

Series 10, episode 2

First transmitted: 14 October 2007

Filming locations: Sidcup, Kent; Dover, Kent; the English Channel; Sangatte, France.

NORMALLY *Top Gear* tries something, makes a bit of a hash of it and then moves on. But with amphibious cars, the producers thought Jeremy, Richard and James had made such a royal cock-up of things that they should try again, and try harder. So, a year or so after the original challenge, they were sent away to have another go. Despite the obvious failings of their original ideas, all three stuck with the same concepts, albeit with a few modifications. Jeremy went for a Nissan pick-up this time because it had a fractionally deeper load bed, which, he reasoned, would make it harder for water to lap over its edges. Richard stuck with a Volkswagen camper van, but also had to buy a new car because his old one had got all wet and was

ruined. James, however, did not replace his Herald because his was the only amphibious car not to get soaked during the original challenge. Also, he rather liked it.

Clarkson's aquatic modifications were a little more thorough this time around, including more comprehensive leak proofing and a pair of barrels that could be swung over the sides to aid stability.

Hammond's re-engineering had been even more thorough with a new fibreglass hull and, taking a tip from Jeremy and James in the original amphibious item, expanding foam crammed into every cavity to aid buoyancy. May had merely refined his design with a new folding mast and a deployable centreboard. All three presenters were feeling confident, right up until the moment they

discovered the scale of the challenge awaiting them – crossing the English Channel.

Before that, however, they had to cross a bit of Kent, a task at which all of them proved utterly hopeless. Thanks to the vast quantities of foam that all three had shoved into every recess of their cars, their engines were starved of cooling air and the only thing they did more than overheat was catch on fire. Hammond, in particular, was subjected to such pungent clouds of noxious fumes that he began to feel extremely sick long before he got out on the sea.

Still, where they failed at being cars, perhaps they would succeed at being boats. Behind the scenes, the producers had applied to the seagoing version of the DVLA and registered all three amphibious

cars as boats. They'd also consulted a man who organises cross-Channel swimming events and who was therefore used to the challenges that face extremely slow-moving things trying to cross the world's busiest shipping lane. Finally, they'd arranged for two boats to follow each car, one carrying a film crew and one containing divers just in case it all went badly wrong out in deep water.

Apart from that, the presenters were on their own, and the hairiness of this challenge shouldn't be underestimated. Little wonder they decided to maximise their chances by setting off during the still period between low and high tide known as 'slack water'.

Since that wasn't until the next day, the presenters went to the pub and the production team organised

for the amphibious cars to be parked in Dover for the night, watched over by a pair of security guards. They returned in the morning to find both guards fast asleep in their van. Not that any thieves trying to take the cars would have got very far, either by land or water.

Finally, it was time to take the plunge. The presenters assembled on the vast landing ramp once used by the now defunct cross-Channel hovercraft and drove gingerly into the sea. Almost immediately it became clear that, whilst James's Herald was fine on the glassy calm of a lake, it was utterly hopeless in the gentle swell of Dover harbour. Richard's MkII Dampervan seemed more competent at first but, after almost getting mown down by the Seacat, it began taking on water and

then sank with almost terrifying speed. The rescue boats managed to drag both back to the shore but their amphibious days were over.

Only Jeremy was left in the running, and he had an idea – since his Nissank was working well, could he beat the Channel-crossing record for amphibious cars set by Richard 'Beardy' Branson back in 2004? There was only one way to find out. With

Hammond and May on board and the sea ahead looking much calmer, Clarkson went for it.

At this point, *Top Gear*'s producers had no idea what would happen next. They'd optimistically sent a camera crew to northern France so that if any of the craft made it they could be filmed arriving on French soil, yet it still seemed most likely that the final shots of the film would be of the white pick-up

On the optimistic assumption that they would actually make it to France, each presenter had to remember to bring their passport with them, as otherwise there was a risk they would have arrived at the other side only to be told to turn around and go straight home again.

truck sinking into the briny or getting liquidised by the propellers of a 50,000-ton cargo ship.

Out of courtesy, the production team had also told the coastguard what was going on and they had breezily promised to fly past in their patrol plane at some point to see how things were going. Sure enough, as the Nissank ploughed on through open water, a small aircraft was seen overhead. As

it turned out, this wasn't the coastguard at all but an airbourne paparazzo who had got word that *Top Gear* was up to something in the Channel and rented a light aircraft to take some pictures. When the actual coastguard swung by they came in so unexpectedly and unbelievably low that you can hear the presenters' genuine exclamations of surprise. With France in sight, the sea got rougher and it looked like it could all be over for Jeremy's bold record attempt. But with some frantic bailing and a welcome calming of the waves nearer land it started to look like they'd actually make it. The film unit on French soil was scrambled to the likely landing point and were there to capture the moment that the pick-up heaved through the waves and made an attempted landing, spitting Hammond overboard and almost crashing down on top of him as it did so. With the aid of a rope and some burly men, the Nissank eventually made it to shore. It hadn't beaten Beardy's record but the fact that it had made it at all was nothing short of extraordinary. In light of this success, the producers didn't feel the need to make the presenters have a third crack at amphibious cars.

THE ALFA ROMEO CHALLENGE

Series II, episode 3

First transmitted: 6 July 2008

Filming locations: Babraham, Cambridgeshire;
Rockingham circuit, Northamptonshire;
the Top Gear Technology Centre, Didcot, Oxfordshire;
Stanford Hall, Leicestershire.

THE Alfa Romeo challenge was inspired by the presenters' long-held belief that you can't be a petrolhead unless you've owned an Alfa Romeo. And when the producers called their bluff on this mantra with a £1,000 challenge, they each took a rather different approach.

Jeremy went for Alfa's last rear-wheel drive saloon, the 75, and kept banging on about things like 'perfect weight distribution' and 'racing pedigree'. James took an unusually modern tack with a 1990s GTV and glossed over the reason for its surprisingly low price, which turned out to be the completely knackered clutch. Richard took the classic route by buying an example of the iconic Spider. Actually, he bought TWO examples of the iconic Spider. The first turned out to be so rotten it was basically a massive pile of Spider-shaped rust held together with paint. As soon as *Top Gear*'s tame mechanic saw this horror he labelled it a death trap and Hammond had to persuade the producers to let him buy another Spider. You can see his original, hopeless purchase in the back of shot at the start of the police car challenge, also from series 11. Frankly, the silver car he ended up with was barely any better.

The challenges here were based on those issued in the cheap Porsches item from series 5, but amped

up a bit. So instead of track tests at the *Top Gear* airfield, they were at a proper circuit in front of other people, thereby cementing the presenters' humiliation when – inevitably – something went wrong. Likewise, the producers had always enjoyed the squirming embarrassment and childish excuses of the concours inspection during the Porsche item, so why not increase that discomfort by doing it not in private at Dunsfold but before a disdainful crowd of experts and Italian car fans? The requirement for each presenter to make a calendar featuring their car was a new idea and – with precisely zero calendars sold – one that went rather badly. If you went into WH Smith in Hammersmith during June 2008 and were baffled as to why they were selling three different and equally dismal calendars featuring hopeless photos of hopeless Alfas, now you know the reason.

All in all, these cruel and unusual challenges worked well and proved that, whilst there's nothing wrong with buying an Alfa Romeo per se, it's probably a good idea to spend more than £1,000 on it. And to keep Jeremy Clarkson away from it.

MERCEDES S-CLASS COTTAGE

Series 8, episode 4

First transmitted: 28 May 2006

Filming locations: London; High Wycombe, Buckinghamshire; the Top Gear test track, Surrey.

FOR as long as anyone could remember, Jeremy had been banging on about the state of car interiors and wondering why they were always made of materials you wouldn't have in your house. Finally, with the arrival of a new Mercedes S-class he'd had enough. This ruched leather and unconvincing plasti-wood obsession must end, and Clarkson would lead the charge by creating his perfect car interior inside an old Merc S280 bought cheaply from the classifieds. In an attempt to be supportive, the *Top Gear* production team found a French interior designer for Jeremy to work with. Unfortunately, her

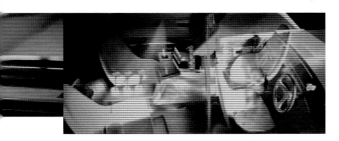

ideas – which were very modern – did not sit well with Clarkson's ideas – which were all based around the interior of his actual house in the Cotswolds. The designer plugged on with her crisply modern, 21st-century designs whilst Jeremy refused to deviate from his plan to, as he put it, 'quaint my ride'. A frosty atmosphere quickly developed. There were several arguments. Jeremy might have accidentally told the French lady that this was 'why you gave in during the war'. Eventually the designer gave in and the insane Rosbif hired a gang of Polish builders to bring his neo-Georgian vision to life. A tame car mechanic was on

hand to step in every time they were about to wallop a nail through one of the side airbags.

Eventually, Jeremy's remodelled S-class was ready. Superficially, it looked rather nice inside, what with the stone flooring, the log burner and the wingback chair. You might even have called it inviting. No set dressing here either: it was all real stone, real wood, real books and a real fire. This explains why the poor old Merc sat so low on its springs and took 35.4 seconds to get from nought to 60. Richard and James proved as much when they took it for a test drive. Hammond also discovered that it's rather hard to control a car

TOP FACT

Jeremy choose this shape of S-class not only because it was cheap but also because it was the last of the old fashioned Benzes, famed for their eight year development processes and indestructible build quality. If anything could take being loaded with concrete, wood and idiocy, this could.

when the driver's seat isn't screwed to the floor. To make their uncontrollable flailing even worse, there was a cameraman in there with them, something Richard was rudely reminded of when he toppled over mid-corner and gashed his head open on the mattebox around the lens.

As soon as Richard and James's disastrous test drive was over and the studio links had been filmed, the S-class was dumped outside the *Top Gear* production office and sat there for several weeks because nobody could be bothered to move it. However, many people who walked past noted the interior looked very cosy.

SOUTH AMERICA SPECIAL

Series 14
First transmitted: 27 December 2009
Filming location: Bolivia

HAVING proved in Botswana that you don't need a 4x4, *Top Gear* perversely decided to prove that sometimes you do. And, after staring at a map for a while and picking somewhere that the programme hadn't been before, the venue for the demonstration of this theory would be South America.

Normally when the presenters buy cars for a challenge they get to size them up first, perhaps even spend some time driving them before filming starts in order to get familiar with their faults and foibles. This time things were different. Each presenter was called separately to the *Top Gear* office and shown websites selling cars in Bolivia. Once they'd made their choices, the producers arranged for a man on the ground to collect them and transport them to a loading-point on

the banks of the Amazon where they would be put on a raft. The first time Jeremy, Richard and James would see their cars would be as they floated into view around a bend in the mighty river.

It was a textbook demonstration of the dangers involved in buying a car sight-unseen. Jeremy's Range Rover did not feature the 3.9-litre engine claimed in the ad. James's Suzuki wasn't even the same colour as the car he'd picked online. And whilst the advert for Richard's Toyota didn't specifically claim that the engine, suspension or brakes worked, it also signally failed to point out that they didn't. Many breakdowns and calamities resulted, but it's only now that the full misery of filming this special can be revealed.

For starters, the presenters' blithering ineptitude at getting their cars off the raft meant that even setting

off took far longer than it should have done, and that meant even more time camping in the hot, sticky and insect-infested rainforest. Nature programmes are always happy to tell you about the diversity of wildlife here, but they never mention how the countless species of monkeys, birds and crawly things make such a racket that it is literally the noisiest place on the planet and, therefore, almost impossible to sleep in. Attenborough also never mentions that as you emerge from the rainforest, there is a chance your film unit will be pursued by a local minor-league drug lord who will attempt to extort money from you with threats of infiltrating your camp at night and murdering your entire production team. Although given a choice, most of the team would have chosen death as a blessed alternative to lying there deafened,

sweaty and wondering what was crawling up their leg. Sleep-deprived and slightly scared, the plucky *Top Gear* team continued up into the hills and onto the famous Death Road. There was no sleight of hand in those shots of Jeremy inching his Range Rover along the very edge of this crumbling hillside pass; it really was that hairy. And worse was to come as darkness fell because Richard and James, constantly delayed by one or both of their cars malfunctioning, simply had to make up time to catch Clarkson. It was too dark to film – the name of the game was simply to get to the next night's camp. Mostly this involved haring down narrow, rough, winding roads with an enormous sheer drop on one side and a series of insanely driven local taxis and badly lit lorries coming the other way. Frankly, it couldn't have been more dangerous. Unless

you were Richard Hammond, whose Land Cruiser had no brakes. It was deeply fortunate that, of the three presenters, Hammond is without question the best driver on loose surfaces. Besides, having to work like Petter Solberg and slow the car almost entirely with the gears took his mind off the things lurking within the nest of jump leads and ropes in the passenger footwell, which he nervously dubbed Spidertown.

Worse was to come when our exhausted duo and their film crews got to that night's stop and encountered a frazzled Clarkson with more bad news. Very close to where they were staying was a bar in which a bigger-league drug baron was hosting a birthday party for his daughter, and music was pumping out at 100 decibels with no sign of stopping much before dawn. In desperation, *Top Gear* executive producer Andy Wilman went into the bar and was soon told that if he made any attempt to turn down the music, he would be 'dealt with'.

The rest of the trip was almost as charming, consisting of great periods of being either extremely hot or uncomfortably cold and at many points driven to the point of breathless insanity by the oxygen deprivation of altitude. All in all, a pretty challenging journey, then. At the end of the trip the presenters flew to Buenos Aires to catch a flight back to London. As they stumbled wearily onto the BA 747 that would take them back to Blighty, one of the cabin crew took a look at James May, his eyes bloodshot, his face unshaven, his hair still caked in dust and sand, and in a one-liner worthy of a Don Draper ad campaign quietly whispered, 'Don't worry, sir, you're almost home.'

10 9 8 7 6 5 4 3 2 1

Published in 2012 by BBC Books, an imprint of Ebury Publishing. A Random House Group company.

Main text by Richard Porter

Copyright © Woodlands Books Ltd 2012

All images © BBC and BBC Worldwide, except p122 and p123 (inset) © Richard Porter

Top Gear (word marks and logos) is a trademark of the British Broadcasting Corporation and used under licence.

Top Gear © 2005

The Random House Group Limited Reg. No. 954009.

Addresses for companies within the Random House Group can be found at www.randomhouse.co.uk

A CIP catalogue record for this book is available from the British Library.

ISBN 978 1 84 990503 9

The Random House Group Limited supports The Forest Stewardship Council (FSC®), the leading international forest certification organisation. Our books carrying the FSC label are printed on FSC® certified paper. FSC is the only forest certification scheme endorsed by the leading environmental organisations, including Greenpeace. Our paper procurement policy can be found at www.randomhouse.co.uk/environment

Commissioning Editor **Lorna Russell**
Project Editor **Joe Cottington**
Copy Editor **Ian Gittins**
Design **Method UK**

Printed and bound in Italy by Printer Trento